Original title:

Umbral Vines Inside the Fae Cask

Author: Sara Säde

ISBN HARDBACK: 978-1-80563-159-0

ISBN PAPERBACK: 978-1-80564-680-8

The Haunting Breath of the Ancient Wild

In shadows deep, the whispers call,
Where ancient trees stand proud and tall.
A shiver dances on the breeze,
As secrets sway among the leaves.

The roots entwined, they softly sing,
Of lost adventures, hidden things.
Their gnarled limbs, a tale they weave,
Of time long past, that will not leave.

Beneath the moon's pale silver light,
The echoes of the forest's night.
With every rustle, spirits roam,
In eerie grace, they find their home.

The haunting breath, a sigh of fate,
Awakens dreams that linger late.
A dance of shadows, flickering bright,
Will guide the lost through veils of night.

Midnight Bloom in the Glistening Hollow

In velvet darkness, petals gleam,
A world awakened from a dream.
The moonlit flowers sway and bow,
In whispered tones, they take their vow.

A fragrance sweet, both rare and fine,
Drifts through the hush, like aged wine.
Their blooms aglow with silver light,
Will lure the stars to share the night.

The glistening hollow, a secret place,
Where time stands still, a warm embrace.
With every breath, enchantments grow,
As midnight's magic starts to flow.

Each blossom holds a tale untold,
Of worlds anew, of dreams of old.
In shimmering hues, they softly bloom,
Illuminating the night's dark gloom.

Whims of the Warding Elderwood

Through tangled paths and sunlight's glare,
The elderwood calls with wisdom rare.
Its branches weave a protective charm,
Guarding the heart with nature's balm.

With every rustle, secrets fly,
A gentle whisper to the sky.
The whims of ages, lost in flight,
Awaken wonders in the night.

A stubborn oak stands tall and proud,
Its leaves adorned in nature's shroud.
With tales of courage, time embraced,
In its deep roots, the past is traced.

The warding elder's ancient grace,
Invites the weary to this place.
Upon its bark, the stories dwell,
Of trials faced and miracles.

Threads of Magic in the Whispering Ferns

In ferns that sway with gentle grace,
Lie threads of magic to embrace.
Their whispering voices weave a spell,
Of curious tales that dance and swell.

Beneath soft canopies, dreams entwine,
In secrets shared by roots and vine.
A sparkle twirls in the evening air,
As faerie laughter drifts everywhere.

Each delicate frond, a cipher bright,
With stories woven through day and night.
In twilight's glow, the magic grows,
Where ferns conceal what no one knows.

Threads of old and threads of new,
Interlace in hues of dew.
A tapestry of life is spun,
In whispering ferns, where all's begun.

Sprites at Dusk in Overgrown Enclaves

In twilight's soft embrace they play,
Tiny whispers on the breeze,
Dancing lights and shadows sway,
Among the leaves of ancient trees.

With gossamer wings, they flit and glide,
Glowing softly, a gentle trace,
In secret glades where dreams reside,
They weave a spell in a sacred space.

The fireflies join their merry throng,
A symphony of twinkling bright,
In harmony, they hum their song,
As day surrenders to the night.

Overgrown paths of emerald hue,
Lead to wonders, lost in time,
Where magic waits in every view,
And hearts beat in a rhythm sublime.

So linger 'neath the twilight's veil,
Embrace the whispers, soft and sweet,
For in their realm, all dreams set sail,
And life becomes a dance, complete.

The Labyrinth of Nocturnal Delights

Winding trails through shadows weave,
A maze of whispers, hushed and low,
Where secrets in the moonlight cleave,
And every turn holds tales to show.

With silver beams that guide the way,
The stars ignite the velvet night,
Each path a promise, bold foray,
To realms untouched by morning's light.

In corners dark, the laughter springs,
Echoes of joy on softest breeze,
As creatures born of night take wing,
They dance amid the swaying trees.

Mirage-like feasts for senses reign,
Sweet nectar drips from fragrant blooms,
In this domain, there's naught but gain,
As magic, brilliant, brightly looms.

So wander forth, embrace the dream,
The labyrinth holds delights untold,
In quiet wonder, life may seem,
A tale awaiting hearts of gold.

Shadows and Glories of Backwood Nature

In thickened woods where shadows blend,
The trees stand tall, their stories keen,
Each gust of wind, a nature's friend,
In rustling leaves, a world unseen.

Sunbeams dance on the forest floor,
Their golden touch on mossy stone,
A symphony of life in core,
As rooted wisdom softly moans.

The sprites at play with fleeting grace,
Beneath the boughs of elder oak,
In every nook, a secret place,
Where whispers breathe, and spirits wroke.

From bramble thick to open glade,
Nature conjures with tender might,
In every shadow, glories laid,
A canvas rich in depth and light.

So stroll these paths where wonder lies,
Embrace the thrum of wild and free,
For in these woods, the spirit flies,
And every glance reveals the key.

Phantasms Draped in Verdant Silks

In emerald depths where phantoms sway,
With silken threads that shimmer bright,
They weave the dusk, a grand ballet,
Their laughter paints the starry night.

Upon soft mists, their forms emerge,
In tangled vines, they softly play,
A tapestry of dreams converge,
Where twilight's whispers stir the day.

With shades of green, they drape the trees,
Adorning nature's gentle frame,
Their presence felt upon the breeze,
A fleeting echo, wild yet tame.

In every rustle, magic stirs,
As shadows twine with moonlight's gleam,
In verdant wraps, the spirit purrs,
Inviting hearts to drift in dream.

So roam where phantasms softly thread,
Among the ferns and blooms that twirl,
In twilight's hold, let doubt be shed,
For nature's dance is life's own pearl.

A Dance Among Shadowed Tendrils

In twilight's grasp, the shadows sway,
Beneath the moon's soft silver ray.
Whispers call with gentle grace,
Inviting hearts to join the chase.

The tendrils twist, a silent scene,
Where secrets hide and dreams convene.
Each step a heartbeat, slow and bold,
In mystic paths of stories untold.

A flicker bursts, the night ignites,
With laughter rippling, sparking lights.
Dancers twirl with spirits free,
In the shimmer of dark harmony.

The forest breathes a magic sound,
As silhouettes waltz 'round and 'round.
In shadows deep where echoes blend,
This dance of night shall never end.

So come, dear soul, embrace the night,
And lose yourself in pure delight.
For in this realm of woven dreams,
The heart finds joy, or so it seems.

Glimmers in the Depths of Green

Amidst the leaves, where sunlight beams,
Awake, the earth reveals her dreams.
A whisper soft, a breeze so sweet,
In emerald depths, where shadows meet.

Glimmers dance in morning's grace,
Among the boughs, the hidden space.
With faeries' smiles and laughter's ring,
The forest wakes, the creatures sing.

In every nook, new wonders bloom,
As nature sheds her weary gloom.
The vibrant hues, a painter's brush,
In this lush world, the heart shall rush.

The tendrils curl like gentle vines,
With every corner, life entwines.
Amongst the roots, where stories lie,
A tapestry 'neath the cobalt sky.

So take a moment, breathe it in,
This living art, a world akin.
For in the depths of green so pure,
Lies magic vast and whispers sure.

The Glistening Path of Hidden Trails

Through tangled woods, a path does gleam,
A secret way, a wanderer's dream.
Each step a spark, where wonders glow,
Upon the trails that few may know.

The mist enfolds the ancient trees,
While nature hums with playful breeze.
With every twist, the heart does race,
In every shadow, a hidden face.

A bridge of light, where glimpses hide,
Invites the brave to step inside.
To follow whispers, soft and low,
Beyond the thickets, truths will flow.

Each moment glistens, each breath a gift,
Along this path, the spirits lift.
With joy and wonder held so dear,
The magic calls—a song to hear.

So wander forth, embrace the land,
To tread the trails that fate has planned.
For here, in stillness, souls shall sail,
Upon the glistening hidden trail.

Threads of Mystique in Nettle Halls

In nettle halls, where shadows weave,
The ancient stories softly breathe.
Each thorny stem, a guardian bold,
In the twilight air, their secrets told.

The whispers wrap with silken threads,
Within the grove, where silence spreads.
A subtle charm, a lace of night,
Enfolds the heart in mystic light.

With every step, the magic swirls,
In hidden realms as time unfurls.
A mystery penned in emerald hues,
Where lost souls find the path they choose.

Through tangled roots and soft decay,
The tendrils lead the heart astray.
Yet in the dark, a spark ignites,
Lighting the way to wondrous sights.

So linger here, amidst the throng,
Where each sweet note becomes a song.
In nettle halls, let spirits crawl,
For life's true beauty resides in all.

Fables Bound in Greenish Gloom

In shadows deep where whispers blend,
Old fables roam, their truths suspend.
Among the leaves, the secrets sigh,
While twilight's breath begins to fly.

Beneath the boughs, the lost ones tread,
In tales that linger long since dead.
The mist encircles, softly sways,
As dreams are caught in dusk's embrace.

Each echo speaks of hearts once bold,
Of legends written, whispered, told.
Yet in the gloom, a spark ignites,
To light the path on starlit nights.

Thus, wanderers seek in silent night,
The fables that elude their sight.
In emerald gloom, the stories swell,
Binding each fate with lingering spell.

And so, they tread through tangled wood,
Embracing all as best they could.
For in the dark where shadows loom,
Lie fables bound in greenish gloom.

The Hidden Orchard of Star-Spun Dreams

In moonlit glades where whispers call,
An orchard thrives beyond the hall.
With fruit as bright as twilight's gleam,
It cradles hope in every dream.

Among the branches, stories dance,
Each petal holds a secret chance.
The air is thick with magic's spell,
In dreams where time itself can dwell.

Beneath the stars, the shadows play,
While night unfolds its rich display.
And there within the velvet shade,
The star-spun dreams are gently laid.

With whispered wishes on the wind,
Each heartbeat sways, and secrets blend.
An orchard dwells where wishes bloom,
A hidden realm amidst the gloom.

So let us wander, hand in hand,
Through this enchanted, timeless land.
For here, where fantasy is sewn,
The star-spun dreams are ours alone.

Secrets Entwined in Nature's Grasp

Amidst the roots, where shadows grow,
A tapestry of secrets flow.
Each leaf a page, each branch a tale,
In nature's grasp, where whispers sail.

The brook's soft sigh weaves through the night,
Revealing truths in silver light.
While ancient oaks stand tall and wise,
Guarding the past beneath the skies.

In twilight's hand, the world unfolds,
With stories wrapped in marigold.
The petals fall with every sigh,
As laughter dances on the sky.

The fluttering wings of twilight's grace,
Each creature knows its sacred place.
Entwined in dreams where shadows cast,
The secrets echo from the past.

So let us wander, hearts attuned,
To nature's breath and beauty crooned.
For in her arms, the world's embrace,
Holds secrets entwined in time and space.

The Dance of Silhouettes in Verdurous Night

As night descends, the world takes flight,
In the dance of silhouettes, so light.
With shadows twirling, spirits roam,
The verdurous night, their ancient home.

Beneath the stars, they sway and spin,
In laughter's glow, a joy within.
The cool, crisp air imbues the soul,
With whispers soft, they lose control.

Each figure bends with nature's sway,
As dreams take shape and drift away.
In moonlit harmony, they play,
Unraveling the night's ballet.

The forest hums with soft delight,
As shadows dance in pure respite.
The heartbeats pulse to nature's beat,
While echoes roam on nimble feet.

So let us join this mystic jest,
Beneath the stars, where spirits rest.
In every corner of the night,
The dance of silhouettes ignites.

Ethereal Blooms Beneath the Starlit Veil

In the hush of night's embrace,
Petals sigh in soft repose,
Glistening with silver lace,
Whispers where the moonlight glows.

Fragile dreams in twilight wait,
Floating on a gentle breeze,
Hand in hand with fate's own gait,
Dancing 'neath the ancient trees.

Luminous the shadows play,
Guided by the starry glow,
Echoes of the twilight sway,
Where the secret wildflowers grow.

Beneath a realm of endless night,
Hope is woven into bloom,
Cradled softly in starlight,
A bloom that banishes all gloom.

In the depths where wonders weave,
Nature sings a haunting tune,
In each heart, we dare believe,
Ethereal blooms beneath the moon.

The Confluence of Night and Verdant Dreams

In twilight's hush, where shadows blend,
The forest breathes in whispered tones,
A tapestry where hopes ascend,
As starlit paths meet mossy stones.

The river's song, a gentle guide,
Winding soft through emerald boughs,
Where secrets of the night abide,
And time bestirs, yet gently bows.

Each rustling leaf a tale reborn,
In silver glances of the moon,
Where dreams are nurtured, whispered, worn,
And echo on like ancient runes.

Yet morning treads on shadow's grace,
With tendrils of a golden hue,
The night retreats, a soft embrace,
While verdant dreams weave visions new.

As stars fade out and dawn takes flight,
The world transforms in radiant streams,
In the confluence of day and night,
We find our truth within our dreams.

Sylvan Whispers from the Darkened Glade

In mysteries of emerald depth,
Where twilight weaves its silken thread,
Soft whispers stir with gentle breath,
In the glade where shadows tread.

The ancient oaks, with arms outspread,
Guard secrets lost through endless time,
While moonbeams rest their golden head,
And crickets hum a lullaby rhyme.

Each rustling blade and silent sigh,
Tells tales of love, of loss, of cheer,
A chorus heard beneath the sky,
Where sylvan spirits linger near.

As night descends with velvet grace,
The glade awakens, soft and bright,
In every corner, hidden space,
Whispers entwine with the fading light.

And so in darkness, life unfolds,
Tales woven in shadows' embrace,
Sylvan whispers, gently told,
In the stillness of this sacred place.

Secrets of the Fern-Laden Hollow

In the hollow kissed by dew,
Where ferns reach high to touch the skies,
A realm of emerald shades anew,
Holds secrets wrapped in nature's sighs.

Beneath the canopy's sweet breath,
The whispers of the past remain,
While fragile lives dance close to death,
And joy and sorrow intertwine.

A hidden world, both strange and bright,
Where sunlight dapples through the trees,
And every echo, every light,
Tells stories swayed by summer's breeze.

The brook, a mirror to the soul,
Trickles softly, secrets shared,
With laughter in each flowing roll,
The hollow hums, forever dared.

In every fern-laden embrace,
Whispers carry, secrets abound,
A sanctuary, a sacred space,
Where nature's heart would ever pound.

Celestial Paths Among Bark and Blossom

Under moonlit skies, the branches sway,
Whispers of magic, in night's soft play.
Stars weave stories 'neath the canopy high,
Where dreams take flight, like birds in the sky.

Each blossom unfurls, a tale to be told,
In twilight's embrace, where the secrets unfold.
The roots hold the wisdom of ages gone by,
As shadows dance gently, and time wanders by.

Winding through groves, where the wildflowers bloom,
Nature's sweet symphony fills every room.
The heart of the forest beats steady and true,
In every twinkling leaf, a love that anew.

In the hush of the night, the cool breeze will sing,
Of journeys and paths that the stars gently bring.
With every soft rustle, a promise we keep,
In the garden of dreams, where the ancient trees weep.

So wander with wonder, and let your heart soar,
Among bark and blossom, there's so much in store.
Find solace in nature, let it guide your way,
In the celestial dance, forever you'll stay.

Dreams Entwined with Faery Winds

In the stillness of dusk, soft whispers arise,
Kissed by the twilight, 'neath indigo skies.
Where faeries flit lightly, on gossamer wings,
They weave through the dreams that the magical brings.

Gentle breezes carry their laughter so sweet,
As shadows grow long, and day's end they greet.
With every soft flutter, the night comes alive,
In a realm where the fanciful truly can thrive.

Through moonbeams and starlight, the wishes take flight,
As dreams interlace with the softest of night.
A tapestry woven with threads of pure light,
Where hope dances freely and hearts feel so bright.

Each sigh of the wind holds a secret untold,
Of lands yet unseen, of treasures and gold.
With faery winds guiding, we find our own way,
In the midst of the magic, forever to stay.

So close your sweet eyes, let your spirit be free,
As you journey through realms only dreamers can see.
Entwined with the faery, where the wild wonders lie,
In the heart of the night, let your dreams truly fly.

Glowworms Carving Paths in the Dark

In the velvet of night, where shadows collide,
Little glowworms shine, like stars in the tide.
They beckon and guide with their soft, gentle light,
Carving out pathways, enchanting the night.

Through the thicket they lead, with a flicker, a glow,
Illuminating secrets that only they know.
Each shimmer a promise, each glint a sweet chance,
To wander through darkness, in nature's soft dance.

Beneath the vast sky, in the stillness we find,
The whispers of ancients, both gentle and kind.
With every soft flicker, forgotten tales rise,
Inviting our hearts to connect with the skies.

The glowworms are guardians, the night lace their thread,

They offer navigation, where few dare to tread.
By their light, we are free, to explore and to dream,
In the warm, tender glow of the night's silver stream.

So follow their twinkle, let your heart feel the spark,
In the embrace of the night, with the glowworms we hark.

Together we'll wander, where shadows meet grace,
Through paths of soft luminous light we will trace.

A Canvas of Leaves and Lore

In the heart of the glade, a canvas unfurls,
Painted with whispers of secrets and swirls.
Leaves rustle softly, each one tells a tale,
Of heroes and journeys, of love's sweet travail.

Where sunlight and shadows play hide and seek,
Every step on the ground speaks volumes, unique.
The stories of old echo through boughs high,
In the dance of the trees, where the spirits fly.

Each leaf holds a token, a chapter once bright,
Of laughter and sorrow, of dreams taking flight.
A tapestry woven from earth's gentle grace,
In the stillness of nature, we all find our place.

The breeze carries scents of the past to the now,
While the rustling branches make solemn a vow.
To cherish each moment, both fleeting and grand,
In this canvas of leaves, where we all understand.

So gather your thoughts, let your spirit embrace,
The stories that linger in this sacred space.
For in every whisper, a new world ignites,
On this canvas of lore, we dance through the nights.

Woven Tales of the Hidden Grove

In whispered woods where secrets dwell,
The ancient trees weave stories well.
With roots that twist and shadows play,
Each leaf a tale, each breeze a sway.

The moonlight drapes a silver shroud,
As creatures dance both meek and proud.
An owl's soft hoot, a nimble throng,
In harmony, they hum their song.

A brook nearby sings gentle rhymes,
Of long-lost loves and forgotten times.
Its waters mirror the starlit skies,
Reflecting dreams in sparkling ties.

Beneath a bough, I sit to dwell,
On woven tales the woods will tell.
In every whisper, in every sigh,
The hidden grove will never die.

So wander forth with heart so light,
And lose yourself in magic's might.
For in the grove, where shadows gleam,
Reality blends with twilight dream.

Resonance Among the Twining Branches

In tangled limbs where whispers cling,
A chorus born from nature's wing.
Resonance rings through air so sweet,
A melody where spirits meet.

The branches twist in playful dance,
Inviting all to join the chance.
A flicker here, a shimmer there,
In harmony we shed our care.

Behold the light that filters through,
Painting the world in emerald hue.
The sunbeams play on forest floor,
Awaking dreams that time restores.

Above, the sky, a canvas wide,
With clouds that drift like thoughts inside.
Each breath a note in nature's score,
A symphony forevermore.

So linger long and hear the call,
Of twining branches, dear to all.
For in this realm, our spirits soar,
In resonance, we become much more.

Fables of the Misty Vale

In mornings draped with silky gray,
The vale awakens, soft and fray.
A tapestry of fog and dreams,
Where every whisper gently gleams.

With every step, a legend sings,
Of hope and loss, of fleeting things.
The echoes swirl like autumn leaves,
Through tangled paths, the heart believes.

By ancient oaks, the fables grow,
In silent thanks, the breezes blow.
Each story holds a spark of light,
That pierces through the veil of night.

A distant horn, a traveler's call,
Resounds within the vale's soft thrall.
And in that sound, a promise made,
That every dawn is not in shade.

So walk this vale with wonder's eyes,
For fables live where magic lies.
In misty shrouds, they weave their part,
A dance of shadow, light, and heart.

The Labyrinthine Heart of the Fae Garden

In secret glades where whispers bloom,
A labyrinth carved by nature's loom.
With petals painted bright and bold,
Each turn a tale of wonders told.

The air is thick with sweet perfume,
As fairies flit in joyful gloom.
With laughter light, they weave a thread,
Through tangled paths where few have tread.

Hidden alcoves, treasures rare,
From ivy wraps and colors fair.
A lantern glows with magic's grace,
In every nook, a smiling face.

Beneath the moon's soft silver kiss,
The garden breathes in tranquil bliss.
So take your time, let wonders chart,
The labyrinthine beats of heart.

For in the depths, true magic lies,
A world alive with ancient ties.
Each step reveals a deeper plan,
In the heart of fae, where dreams began.

Twilit Arbors and Celestial Threads

In twilight's glow the arbors sway,
With whispers soft at end of day.
The stars like seeds in velvet skies,
Bespoke of dreams where magic lies.

Each branch adorned with silver dew,
A tapestry of colors true.
Through leafy lanes, the shadows dance,
Embracing all that holds a chance.

With every sigh, the night unfurls,
And cradles tales of distant worlds.
In every nook a secret hides,
In twilit realms where hope abides.

So wander forth, let heart take flight,
In gardens wrought of pure delight.
Through whispered paths, a realm anew,
Where dreams and starlight weave their view.

Beneath the Canopy of Forgotten Realms

Beneath the arches, ancient, grand,
Lies whispered lore of distant lands.
The canopy, a living dream,
In shadows deep, the fireflies gleam.

The roots embrace the tales untold,
Of heroes brave, of hearts of gold.
Each rustling leaf, a memory,
Of days long past, a reverie.

Here time stands still, a gentle breath,
Where echoes dance and shadows jest.
In every nook, a story waits,
Of timeless love and twisting fates.

So linger close, and breathe it in,
The magic found where dreams begin.
Explore the depths where wonders gleam,
Beneath the light of starlit dreams.

The Midnight Weaving of Enigmatic Flora

In darkness thick, the flowers weave,
A fabric rich, where none believe.
With petals soft, a fragrant sigh,
They spin their tales beneath the sky.

The moonlight bathes each bloom in grace,
In silent dance, they find their place.
A symphony of colors blend,
In midnight's hush, where dreams transcend.

The quivering leaves, a gentle hum,
In secret gardens, magic's drum.
Each blossom whispers ancient lore,
Of life and love forevermore.

So close your eyes, let senses bloom,
In tangled paths of sweet perfume.
Embrace the night, the stars anew,
In midnight's weave, feel dreams come true.

Nocturnal Petals Beneath the Fabled Boughs

Beneath the boughs where shadows play,
Nocturnal petals find their way.
In silence deep, they stretch and yawn,
Each day gives way to shimmering dawn.

They kiss the earth, in soft embrace,
As starlit glimmers trace their grace.
The wonders hidden from the day,
In night's embrace, they softly sway.

Upon the breeze their secrets glide,
While moonbeams dance, unable to hide.
In every fold, a magic found,
Where whispers twine around the ground.

So seek the paths where magic waits,
In wonderous blooms and twisted fates.
Through hidden realms, let spirits soar,
Nocturnal dreams forevermore.

Woven Silhouettes in Celestial Embrace

In twilight's glow, we weave our dreams,
Silhouettes dance, in gentle streams.
Underneath the stars so bright,
Hearts entwined in whispered light.

Clouds drift by, a silver shroud,
Casts shadows deep, our solace proud.
With every breath, the night takes flight,
In celestial embrace, our souls unite.

Through twinkling skies, our hopes ascend,
Woven threads that never end.
Each heartbeat sings, a timeless rhyme,
As we glide through the fabric of time.

Moonlit paths, a tapestry,
Woven silhouettes in harmony.
With every pulse, the cosmos spins,
A dance where love forever begins.

In dreams we find, what we believe,
In starlit fears, we dare to weave.
A journey shared, through vast expanse,
In this embrace, we take our chance.

The Serpent's Kiss Amongst Eldritch Blooms

In the garden, shadows creep,
Where eldritch blooms in silence weep.
A serpent's kiss, both soft and sly,
Beneath the moon, the secrets lie.

Petals whisper ancient lore,
Of magic lost and battles sore.
With emerald eyes that twist and turn,
The spark of life, forever yearn.

Creeping vines entwine the night,
Serpent's breath, a ghostly light.
In shadows deep, where visions dwell,
Know the tales the blooms now tell.

Each petal's touch, a fleeting grace,
An otherworldly, tender embrace.
Amongst the flora, we shall tread,
In haunting dreams, where angels fled.

Eldritch blooms in twilight fade,
Yet still we seek the paths they made.
For in each kiss, a story wakes,
And through the dark, our courage shakes.

Elusive Flora Beyond the Bramble's Watch

Beyond the bramble, secrets hide,
Elusive flora, where dreams reside.
A pathway bold, through thorn and thorn,
We seek the blooms, where hopes are born.

Whispers call from twilight's edge,
A delicate promise, a hidden pledge.
In every rustle, the winds convey,
A map of stars, to guide our way.

Petals soft, like dusk's caress,
In nature's arms, we find our rest.
Beyond the bramble, time stands still,
Where magic flows, and hearts can fill.

The forest breathes, a gentle sigh,
As fleeting shadows drift on by.
In hidden groves, we dare to dream,
Where flora thrives in twilight's gleam.

Through tangled paths, our spirits soar,
In every blossom, we must explore.
Elusive scents that haunt the night,
Lead us ever, to the light.

The Enigma of Shade-Kissed Foliage

In shaded realms where whispers dwell,
The foliage holds its timeless spell.
Each leaf a tale, each branch a song,
Secrets murmured, where we belong.

Beneath the boughs, the shadows play,
In dappled light, they drift away.
With every breeze, a mystery stirs,
A dance of thoughts that softly purrs.

Shade-kissed trails in emerald hues,
Guide wandering souls on paths we choose.
In tangled roots, the past remains,
An enigma wrapped in nature's chains.

With every step on mossy floors,
We delve into the hidden doors.
Where silence speaks and hearts entwine,
In shade-kissed foliage, we find the divine.

A world alive, with dreams anew,
In every glimmer, a chance to pursue.
In nature's heart, the echoes call,
In shaded realms, we find our all.

Shadowed Canopies and Elfin Laughter

In twilight's hold, the shadows play,
Beneath the trees where fairies sway.
Whispers soft as silken threads,
In secret glades where magic bled.

The moonlight filters through the leaves,
As laughter stirs, the heart believes.
A dance of spirits, light and free,
In hidden nooks of mystery.

With every giggle, echoes rise,
A symphony of starlit skies.
The ancient trees, with gnarled roots,
Keep tales of love and playful flutes.

In emerald hues, the secrets lie,
Where dreams are born and gently sigh.
A hush falls over twilight's breath,
As fairies weave the dreams of depth.

So wander forth, with heart aglow,
In shadowed canopies, let go.
Elfin laughter beckons near,
In these lush woods, have no fear.

The Cryptic Dance of Veiled Blossoms

A moonlit path of glimmering dew,
Awakens blooms with secrets new.
In twilight's grasp, they sway and twirl,
Draped in veils of softest pearl.

Petals whisper in the hushed night,
In cryptic dance, a fleeting sight.
Colors blend in twilight's grace,
As shadows hide in a gentle embrace.

With every swirl, a tale unfolds,
Of love and loss in petals bold.
The garden hums a haunting song,
Where mysteries of dusk belong.

The fragrant air, a woven spell,
Captures hearts where secrets dwell.
In twinkling light, the flowers sing,
Of ancient joy that spring can bring.

So step within this world divine,
Where veiled blossoms intertwine.
The dance of night reveals the past,
In cryptic tales forever cast.

Lurking Spirits amid Leafy Patterns

Underneath the verdant shade,
Where sun and shadow intertwine laid.
The spirits linger, veiled yet near,
In leafy patterns, whispers clear.

Soft rustles greet the wandering soul,
As branches weave a quiet toll.
Amidst the ferns, old echoes dwell,
In leafy patterns, stories tell.

A flicker here, a shimmer there,
In emerald depths, they fill the air.
Secrets breathe in every sigh,
As guardians watch with ancient eye.

With every step, the senses wane,
In twilight's hush, a spectral reign.
Their laughter rings from roots below,
In leafy patterns, spirits glow.

Embrace the realms where shadows rest,
And find the place your heart loves best.
For lurking spirits, wise and kind,
Bring dreams to those who seek and find.

The Initiation of the Hidden Grove

In tangled vines, a pathway lies,
Where whispers rise to greet the skies.
The hidden grove, a sacred place,
Awaits the seeker's gentle grace.

With every footstep, magic blooms,
In fragrant air that softly looms.
The trees, they beckon, tall and wise,
In initiation, watch spirits rise.

A circle forms of ancient wood,
In silent pact, where dreams once stood.
Light flickers in an emerald hue,
The grove reveals what's meant for you.

Through mossy paths, the heart draws near,
To touch the wonders, quell the fear.
In every rustle, secrets flow,
This sacred rite of the hidden grove.

So wander forth, with spirit bright,
Embrace the magic of the night.
For in this grove, your soul shall learn,
The ancient truths for which you yearn.

The Enchanted Choir of the Nether Tree

In twilight's hush they blend and weave,
The voices rise, both sweet and grave.
From branches high, a chorus sings,
Of hidden realms and ancient wings.

Each note, a tale of magic bright,
Of whispered dreams and endless night.
The moonlight dances on their song,
A lullaby where hearts belong.

With every breeze, the leaves do sway,
Inviting souls to pause and stay.
A gathering of spirits bold,
In harmonies that never grow old.

The stars lean close, to hear them call,
In shadows deep, where whispers fall.
The enchantment grows, a spell we share,
In melodies that linger there.

Together bound in nature's grace,
They paint the night with soft embrace.
In every heart, their echoes dwell,
The Nether Tree, where magic swells.

Veils of Dappled Shade and Light

Through leafy boughs the sunlight streams,
In patterns soft like lullaby dreams.
Whispers float on gentle air,
Companions found in branches rare.

The forest breathes, alive with grace,
A hidden world, a sacred place.
Each step reveals a secret bloom,
As shadows dance, dispelling gloom.

With every gust, the colors shift,
A fleeting gift, a nature's lift.
In harmony, the hues embrace,
Veils of magic, time can't erase.

The rustling leaves, a soft refrain,
Invite the heart to feel the rain.
Where stillness reigns, the spirit finds,
A tapestry woven in kinds.

As dusk descends, the peace unfolds,
In whispered tones, the story told.
Veils of shade and light conspire,
To spark the soul with quiet fire.

Blossoms Swept by the Winds of Myth

The petals fall like whispered dreams,
Carried forth on wandering streams.
In every breeze a tale takes flight,
Of ancient lore, of day and night.

The world awakes with colors bright,
As blossoms sway in sheer delight.
Each bloom a chapter, soft and kind,
Of tales once lost to time's cruel bind.

In fragrant scents, the stories rise,
Like stars that twinkle in the skies.
The myths are woven in the air,
Reminders that we all must care.

With every gust, the legends whirl,
As blossoms dance, and fates unfurl.
The whispers speak of paths unclear,
Yet promise dreams will always steer.

Together bound by nature's hand,
They sway and twirl in magic land.
The winds of myth, a gentle guide,
Where past and present coincide.

Murmurs of the Shrouded Glade

In hidden nooks where shadows play,
The murmur softens night and day.
Among the trees, a secret throng,
A place where whispers do belong.

The mossy floor, a sturdy bed,
Where dreams of old are gently spread.
A haven found, in silence deep,
Where ancient spirits seem to sleep.

The twilight hum, a soothing sound,
In every breath, the past is found.
With every rustle, echoes swell,
In voices low, they weave a spell.

The glade holds tales of time gone by,
Underneath the vast, starlit sky.
Murmurs stir like softest lace,
A tapestry of time and space.

As night descends, the magic glows,
In every heart, the murmur flows.
In shrouded glades, the memories throng,
Inviting all to join the song.

Tangled Oaths in the Whispering Wood

In the woods where shadows play,
Whispers linger, soft as day.
Oaths are tangled, hearts entwine,
Promises spoken, crossed like a line.

Underneath the ancient trees,
Flickering lights dance in the breeze.
Secrets hide in roots so deep,
Guarding dreams that time will keep.

Voices echo, lost and found,
In this magic, hope is wound.
Tales of old, yet fresh as dew,
In the laughter, bonds renew.

Branches weave a mystic map,
Where lovers' dreams and shadows nap.
Fated paths converge tonight,
In the woods where wrong feels right.

Stars above in velvet skies,
Glimmer softly, hear the sighs.
Tangled oaths, a sacred blend,
In the wood, where hearts transcend.

Roots Beneath the Veil of Starlight

Beneath the stars, roots intertwine,
Whispering secrets, old as time.
Veils of night drape o'er the earth,
While dreams take flight, embrace their worth.

Moonlight weaves through branches bare,
Crickets sing of love and care.
In the hush, the world stands still,
Awakening dreams, like magic thrill.

Softly now, the shadows wane,
Dancing in an age-old rain.
With every heartbeat, they bestow,
Wisdoms woven, time shall sow.

The stars, they wink, a cosmic jest,
Binding threads of fate and quest.
Each spark a wish that travels far,
Guiding souls like a steadfast star.

Roots beneath where starlight sighs,
Hold the tales of ages, wise.
Underneath this vast expanse,
We find ourselves in cosmic dance.

The Wraith's Serenade in the Bushy Realm

In the bushy realm where wraiths reside,
Ghostly figures in twilight bide.
Silent songs float on the breeze,
Caressing hearts with haunting ease.

Lanterns flicker, spirits tread,
Whispers dance of wishes dead.
With each note, a story spins,
Echoes of what could have been.

Veils of mist like dreams conceal,
Within the night, emotions heal.
Sorrow mingles with the light,
Creating tapestry of night.

Shadows beckon, soft and low,
In their grasp, we come to know.
The wraiths hum their melancholic tune,
Underneath the watchful moon.

In this realm where echoes play,
Hearts can wander, drift away.
Amidst the thorns, the sorrowed wraiths,
Sing their serenade of fates.

The Forbidden Path Among the Thickets

Amidst the thickets, shadows loom,
Forbidden paths, an air of gloom.
Once bright hopes now tangled tight,
Woven deep in the cloak of night.

Echoes haunt the weary soul,
Tales of loss take a heavy toll.
Yet every heart seeks a new dawn,
To break the silence, rise reborn.

Thorns may scratch, and fears may grow,
Yet courage whispers, softly, low.
Step by step, the way unfolds,
As fate reveals what the heart holds.

Through the bramble, light will break,
Shimmering dreams in every ache.
Paths forbidden, now be embraced,
In the journey, wisdom traced.

Amidst the thickets, hope shall thrive,
Finding ways to come alive.
The heart knows well the crooked route,
Among the thickets, in fear, we sprout.

Eclipsed Echoes of Twisted Roots

In the forest where time softly bends,
Whispers linger where the darkness descends.
Twisted roots curl beneath the pale light,
Echoes of stories lost to the night.

A voice in the shadows, a faint lullaby,
Secrets entwined in the breath of a sigh.
Branches stretch out like fingers of fate,
Reaching for dreams that lie in wait.

Each rustle of leaves holds a tale to unfold,
Of hearts intertwined and the bravest of souls.
In the silence, a pulse beats in tune,
With the magic that dances beneath the moon.

Eclipsed by the sorrow, yet glimmers of hope,
In the tangled embrace where the lost learn to cope.
Roots buried deep in the earth's warm embrace,
Whispering love in a timeless space.

As shadows take form, a soft silver hue,
Awakens the secrets that linger in dew.
Resilient and strong, the echoes will sing,
Of lives once entwined, of time's gentle swing.

Whispered Secrets in the Moonlit Grove

In a grove where the moon weaves its soft spell,
Lies a whispering tide, an enchanting swell.
Branches sigh low with secrets untold,
In shadows they linger, in glimmers of gold.

The owls call softly, their voices a thread,
In the tapestry woven where dreams dare to tread.
Each flick of a wing stirs the essence of night,
Revealing the magic, elusive yet bright.

Glittering lights twinkle like stars in disguise,
While whispers of wonder drift high to the skies.
In the heart of the grove, time slips through our hands,
As we dance with the shadows, in forgotten lands.

Secrets entwined with the roots of the trees,
Carried by breezes, a gentle tease.
The moon's silver glow casts a shimmering lace,
Over lovers who wander, lost in the space.

So let the night wrap us in its tender embrace,
A haven of whispers, a hushed, sacred place.
For in these shadows, the heart finds its song,
In whispered secrets, we forever belong.

The Gossamer Tangle of Shadows' Embrace

In the twilight's dim glow, shadows entwine,
Gossamer threads of the past combine.
A tapestry woven from laughter and tears,
In the embrace of the darkness, we conquer our fears.

Each flicker of light, like a star in the night,
Guides us through whispers, igniting our flight.
Through the tangled embrace of life's fragile loom,
We dance with the phantoms, as they carve our gloom.

With every soft step, the echoes revive,
Lost dreams of the heart, clutching threads to survive.
Weaving our stories, with love as our guide,
In the gossamer tangle, we flourish beside.

The shadows may shift, yet they always remain,
Guardians of secrets, of joy and of pain.
As night wraps around us, we'll twirl in delight,
In the embrace of the shadows, we find our true light.

For each whispered sigh and each shimmering glance,
Is a note in the symphony of fate's grand dance.
The gossamer threads are the ties that won't break,
In shadows we flourish, for love's gentle sake.

Enchanted Tendrils of Twilight's Heart

In the dusk where enchantment unfurls its wings,
Tendrils of twilight hum softly and sing.
Misty illusions wrap 'round with a sigh,
Painting the dusk as the stars drift and fly.

With a breath of the evening, the world holds its breath,
In the garden of dreams, where nothing is left.
A dance of the fireflies flits in the air,
Shimmering spells that weave wonder and care.

The horizon ignites in a canvas of hues,
Pastel and bold in the fading day's blues.
Nature's soft canvas, brushed tender and sweet,
Whispers of magic, where shadows repeat.

As the moon softly rises, the night comes alive,
With enchanted tendrils that tug at our drive.
They weave through our hearts, filling voids long ignored,

In twilight's embrace, where souls are restored.

So linger a moment, let the magic unfold,
In the tender twilight, where stories are told.
With each fleeting breath, let curiosity start,
In the enchanted tendrils of twilight's heart.

Enigma of the Twisted Branches

In woods where shadows twist and sway,
Ancient whispers lead the way,
Beneath the gnarled and tangled trees,
Lies a secret carried by the breeze.

Roots entwined, a tale untold,
Of lost worlds and dreams of gold,
Through knotted paths that time forgot,
A trace of magic, tangled, caught.

With every flutter, moss decays,
Echoes linger in the haze,
The branches speak, a silent chant,
To those who question, hope or want.

Behind the bark, a spirit glows,
A riddle blooms where no one knows,
If you listen, you might find,
The heart of nature, intertwined.

So wander forth with open mind,
In twisted branches, truth you'll find,
For in the arcane, magic dwells,
And every secret gently tells.

Folklore of the Starlit Glade

Beneath the canopy, stars ignite,
In glades where dreams take flight,
Fairies dance on leaves of silver,
Their laughter echoes, sweet and shiver.

A brook sings softly to the night,
Echoing tales of forgotten plight,
Of lovers lost and curses spun,
In the shimmering moon, their journey's begun.

The trees, they whisper ancient lore,
Of battles fought on distant shore,
And hearts entwined in twilight's grip,
Held close in shadows, a fated trip.

Fireflies twinkle, a guiding light,
In starlit glades, where day meets night,
And every flicker, a flick of fate,
A map to wonders, love, or hate.

So venture where the shadows play,
In folklore's grasp, let your heart sway,
For in the glade, both dark and bright,
Lie stories waiting for the right night.

Secrets of the Luminous Thicket

In thickets thick with golden light,
Where secrets hide from day and night,
A shimmer dances on each leaf,
A promise wrapped in soft belief.

The ferns, they sway to a quiet tune,
Beneath the watchful gaze of the moon,
Each step brings whispers soft and low,
As ancient magic starts to glow.

Hidden creatures stir awake,
As dreams and truths begin to shake,
A spell unfolds, both sweet and stark,
In luminous depths where shadows hark.

With every breath, the forest sighs,
Each secret told beneath the skies,
And if you pause, you'll hear them speak,
Of paths untraveled, futures bleak.

So venture forth to chase the light,
In thickets where the stars burn bright,
For in the glow, the heart will find,
The whispered secrets of the mind.

The Serpent's Kiss in the Glade

In glades where shadows curl and creep,
The serpent's kiss, a promise deep,
Beneath the canopy, danger lies,
Wrapped in beauty, cloaked in disguise.

With scales that glimmer, emerald bright,
The creature weaves through day and night,
A guardian of the woodland's heart,
Ready to ensnare, to tear apart.

In whispered legends, caution flows,
Where magic lingers, fate bestows,
For every choice comes with a price,
And beauty oft hides in a vice.

Yet in this glade, the truth unfolds,
Not all that glitters can turn to gold,
Through tangled roots, a path is made,
To discover love where fears invade.

So tread with care, for love can sting,
In the serpent's kiss, the heart takes wing,
As twilight dawns and shadows wane,
In glades of magic, love will reign.

Beneath the Canopy of Forgotten Whispers

Beneath the trees where secrets sigh,
Ancient roots entwine the sky.
Whispers dance on the silver breeze,
Lost tales hum with the rustling leaves.

Moonlight spills through branches wide,
Nestling dreams where shadows hide.
Each echo holds a timeless spark,
In the stillness, hear the dark.

Crickets sing their twilight song,
With every note, the night feels long.
Starlit paths in the cool night air,
Guide the heart to the wonders there.

Fingers brush the emerald bracken,
Where time once turned and fate was slackened.
Among the ferns, a tale awaits,
Of love and loss, of twisted fates.

So linger long, let spirits flow,
In whispered tones, the past will glow.
Beneath the canopy, shadows blend,
In magic's grasp, we shall transcend.

The Nightshade's Sweet Lure

In twilight's grasp, the nightshade blooms,
With velvet petals and dark perfumes.
Its sweetness calls with a haunting strain,
Promising bliss and banishing pain.

Beneath the moon's pale, tender gaze,
The heart entangled in a wicked maze.
A lover's touch, both gentle and fierce,
Draws nearer still that longing pierce.

Beware the charm in the dusky glade,
For shadows hide what the light betrayed.
In fragrant dreams, the spirits play,
Enticing whispers lead hearts astray.

The thrumming pulse of passion's piqued,
Yet hidden truths remain mystique.
With every sigh, the danger grows,
On paths where nightshade's allure flows.

Yet in the dark, a promise gleams,
Of fragile hopes and tender dreams.
So dance with fate, though shadows loom,
For love's sweet lure dispels the gloom.

Echoes from the Hidden Glens

In hidden glens where silence lingers,
Nature breathes with tender fingers.
The brook's soft gurgle, the rustle of grass,
Whispers of time as moments pass.

Each echo tells a tale untold,
Of ancient woods and legends bold.
In dappled light where fairies tread,
Dreams awaken in hues of red.

Beneath the boughs, the secrets nest,
Cradled on earth in nature's breast.
With every step, the past resounds,
In sweet refrain from hollowed grounds.

Speak softly now, let silence reign,
Hear the voices of joy and pain.
In every breeze, the heart recalls,
The echoes hidden within the walls.

So wander deep where shadows play,
And let your spirit drift away.
For in the glens, the world will stir,
A symphony of whispers, a gentle purr.

Shadows Weaved with Nature's Lullaby

In twilight's hush, the shadows dance,
Nature croons in a soft expanse.
The cradle of leaves, the hush of night,
Wraps the world in its tender light.

Stars twinkle bright in the velvet air,
While crickets sing without a care.
The moon's embrace, a gentle guide,
Stirs the dreams that in darkness tide.

Soft winds carry a lullaby's note,
While nature's heartbeat begins to float.
With whispers sweet, the night unfolds,
A tapestry of stories told.

Mist swirls low in the moonlit glen,
Where time is lost, again and again.
Among the trees, peace weaves its thread,
As dreams descend upon sleepy heads.

So close your eyes and drift, my dear,
In nature's arms, cast aside your fear.
For shadows weave with love's soft sigh,
In this night's cradle, we shall lie.

Echoes of the Forest's Heartbeat

In shadows deep, the whispers sound,
Of ancient trees and hallowed ground.
With every rustle, tales unfold,
Of guardians wise and secrets old.

The brook sings soft, a lullaby,
While starlit dreams weave through the sky.
Here, friendships bloom in emerald hues,
In the heart of the woods, life's vibrant muse.

Beneath the canopy, time stands still,
Where every breath the forest will.
A heartbeat strong in rhythmic tone,
Calls adventurers to roam alone.

The owls observe with watchful gaze,
Counting the hours in dusky haze.
While ferns sway dancing to the breeze,
With every whisper, a gentle tease.

And as the twilight draws its veil,
The spirits rise, an ancient tale.
Their laughter echoes, sweet and clear,
In the forest's heart, forever near.

Beneath the Cloak of Dusk's Embrace

The twilight wraps the world in gold,
As night unfolds its stories bold.
With creeping shadows, secrets spill,
In every corner, the air is still.

The stars awaken, one by one,
Bathing dreams in silver run.
While whispers travel on the breeze,
In hidden paths through the rustling trees.

Beneath this cloak, the world feels new,
Each moment cherished, each heartbeat true.
The soft glow beckons, inviting in,
To realms where time and magic spin.

The nightingale sings her sweet refrain,
A melody laced with soft perfume.
For in the dusk, all fears dissolve,
Beneath the night, our hearts evolve.

So linger here where wonder lies,
Embrace the darkness, touch the skies.
For under dusk's deep, soothing grace,
We find ourselves in time and space.

The Secret Dance of Forgotten Flora

In hidden glades where shadows play,
The flowers whisper, night and day.
With petals soft, they sway and spin,
To tunes that only they begin.

Each bloom a tale, each color bright,
Reflecting magic born of light.
With trembling leaves, they tell their story,
Of fleeting moments and faded glory.

Their fragrant forms, a dance of old,
In twilight's glow, they brave the cold.
While dew drops glisten, a diamond's tear,
They spin in silence, year to year.

Among the roots, the secrets lie,
Of ancient dreams that linger nigh.
These cherished blooms, though oft ignored,
In moonlit nights, their beauty soared.

So wander forth, discover new,
The hidden paths, the magic too.
For in the dance of flora bound,
The love of nature can be found.

Mysteries of the Hollowed Trunks

In hollowed trunks, the stories sleep,
Of woodland creatures' secrets deep.
Within their rings, an age unfolds,
Whispers of winters and summers cold.

These ancient sentinels stand tall,
Guarding tales of love and fall.
Their bark worn thin, yet strong within,
A legacy where time begins.

With every notch, a mark of life,
Of joys and sorrows, love and strife.
Beneath their shade, the children play,
In laughter's echo, come what may.

Yet mysteries cloak their weathered form,
As nature's storms begin to swarm.
If you listen close, you might hear,
A murmur soft, a voice so near.

So next you pass a tree so grand,
Remember tales, this sacred land.
For in their hearts, the stories lie,
Of every creature darting by.

The Dancer's Shadows Beneath the Grove

In twilight's embrace where the shadows play,
The dancers move with a whispered sway,
Each step a secret, each twirl divine,
In circles of magic, the stars align.

The leaves are their audience, soft and bright,
As moonlight glimmers, casting gentle light,
Footfalls of fairies, light as a sigh,
In this hidden grove where dreams fly high.

Veils of laughter trace the evening air,
In shadows they gather, without a care,
The heartbeat of nature, a silent song,
In timeless rhythm, where we belong.

With every twirl, the night deepens still,
As magic unfurls, time bends to their will,
A dance of enchantment, boundless and free,
In the heart of the grove, they call unto me.

So come, take my hand; let us weave through time,
In the dancer's shadows, all will be fine,
For here in the twilight, with spirits so bold,
The stories of ages in secrets unfold.

Fae Lights Flickering in Twilight Veil

Through the twilight's hush where the fae lights gleam,
In gentle whispers, they weave a dream,
Soft glimmers dancing, where shadows entwine,
In the heart of the night, their magic aligns.

Each flicker a tale, by starlight rehearsed,
Of secrets and wishes, of love, and of thirst,
The flickering glow that guides lost souls,
Through pathways of silence, where moonlight rolls.

Their laughter, a melody, sweet as a stream,
In the cradle of night, where wonders redeem,
A symphony woven of laughter and care,
With every soft flutter, they vanish, they dare.

As shadows grow long and the world hugs the night,
With fae lights a-twinkle, a whimsical sight,
I follow their trail, as the stars start to sway,
In the twilight's embrace, where dreams find their way.

Oh, to dance with the fae and to soar without sound,
In the twilight's veil where enchantments abound,
For time holds no power in this sacred ground,
With fae lights flickering, true joy can be found.

The Shimmering Web of Woodland Tales

In the heart of the forest where secrets abide,
A shimmering web spins time far and wide,
With threads of the past, so rich and so deep,
It captures the whispers the ancients keep.

Each glimmering strand tells a story profound,
Of creatures and magic in sacred surround,
From the rustle of leaves to the brook's gentle sigh,
In the shimmering web, the lost tales don't die.

Catch a glimpse of the fairies, their laughter in flight,
As day turns to dusk in a dance of pure light,
With every new thread, a new saga appears,
Woven through ages, transcending the years.

The woodland awakens, as mysteries flare,
In the weave of the tales, rich beyond compare,
The shimmer invites us, with promises bright,
To listen, to learn, in the quiet of night.

So come gather around, let the stories unfold,
In the shimmering web, where the heart turns to gold,
For in every flicker, in every soft sigh,
The woodland's own magic will never say die.

Whispers of the Mossy Underworld

Beneath ancient boughs where the shadows reside,
The whispers of moss in the damp earth confide,
Tales of the ages, in hushed, reverent tone,
Of secrets and dreams that the wild things have known.

Here roots intertwine, in a dance so discreet,
With stories of life woven down at our feet,
The echoes of footsteps in long-forgotten lore,
Guide us to places we've never explored.

The stillness enchants, as if time holds its breath,
In the mossy confines of silence and depth,
Each rustle, a promise, each murmur, a name,
In the underworld's heart where the wild spirits flame.

Feel the pulse of the earth, let your worries disperse,
In the whispering moss, where the shadows converse,
With gentle reminders of magic unseen,
In the forest's embrace, where all of us dream.

So wander with me, down the paths of the old,
Through whispers of moss, let the stories unfold,
For beneath every frond, and each covered stone,
Lies the essence of life, in the earth's gentle tone.

Nocturnal Chants of the Gloom

In shadows deep where whispers dwell,
The secrets crawl, the sorrows swell.
Beneath the stars, a muted moan,
The night reveals its darker tone.

A chill winds weave through silent trees,
Eerie echoes borne by the breeze.
Lost souls gather, their tales they share,
In twilight's grip, they breathe despair.

The moon hangs low, a watchful eye,
While solemn shadows wane and sigh.
In the gloaming, shapes entwine,
A symphony of dark divine.

A lantern's light flickers and fades,
Mysteries wrapped in velvet shades.
The gloom sings loud, it will not fade,
A haunting dance, a spell is laid.

An ancient pact in silence sworn,
From dusk's embrace, the spirits mourn.
In glooms, their baleful voices rise,
With nocturnal chants that pierce the skies.

Moonlit Vines and Celestial Whirls

In gardens where the moonlight spills,
The vines entwine with whispered thrills.
Stars twinkle bright, with secrets shared,
In this haven, no heart is scared.

Beneath the glow, the petals dance,
In swirling revelries, they prance.
The nightingale lifts sweet refrain,
In harmony with joy and pain.

Through silver strands, let shadows weave,
In tapestry of night, believe.
A dream unfolds in soft embrace,
With cosmic waltzes, time and space.

The air is thick with fragrant sighs,
As nature hums and softly cries.
Twilight brings a gentle charm,
Where vines entwined keep spirits warm.

As constellations spin and gleam,
In moonlit realms, we drift and dream.
With every breath, the world awakes,
In whispers sweet, the night partakes.

The Fairone's Lament in the Underbrush

Beneath the boughs where willows weep,
A fairone sings, her heart does leap.
In tangled roots, her sorrows flow,
Among the brambles, soft and slow.

Her voice, a melody of grief,
That echoes through the leafy sheaf.
With every note, the wildflowers bend,
In quiet homage, they do attend.

The moon casts shadows on her face,
As memories fill this resting place.
Longing haunts her in dusk's embrace,
For love once lost, a bitter trace.

The thorns betray her gentle touch,
Yet in the light, she longs so much.
For echoes of a sweeter past,
In tangled dreams, the die is cast.

With every tear that falls like dew,
A song of fate, her heart's adieu.
In the underbrush, her tale resounds,
A fairone's lament in sacred grounds.

Dance of the Eldritch Flora

In moonlit woods where shadows play,
The flora twirls in mystic sway.
Their petals hum with ancient lore,
In silent whispers, secrets pour.

The ground alive with emerald hue,
As eldritch roots entwine anew.
Their dance, a ritual of the night,
In fragrant dreams, they take their flight.

From ferns that flicker to blooms that gleam,
A symphony of nature's dream.
With every step on softest earth,
The flowers pulse with boundless mirth.

A canopy of stardust weaves,
In this enchanted world, believes.
While moonlight casts its silver spell,
In harmony, they weave and dwell.

With every breeze, their chorus swells,
Within the woods, where magic dwells.
So dance, dear heart, let shadows twine,
For in their steps, the stars align.

Whispers of Twilight Canopy

In twilight's hush, the whispers sing,
'Neath leaves aglow, the soft winds bring.
A secret dance of dusk and dawn,
Where dreams take flight and fears are gone.

The branches sway, a gentle grace,
With shadows weaving, a hidden place.
The stars appear, a silver shroud,
Encased in night, the forest proud.

Moonlight fills the silent air,
With magic weaving everywhere.
A fleeting thought, a fleeting glance,
In twilight's arms, we take our chance.

Each rustle speaks of tales untold,
Of creatures bold and hearts of gold.
In whispered tones, the stars do sigh,
As night unfolds the dreamer's eye.

The canopy holds mysteries tight,
As we embrace the tender night.
In shadows deep, our spirits soar,
In whispers of the twilight lore.

Enchanted Roots in Moonlit Grotto

Beneath the boughs, the roots entwine,
In moonlit glow, their secrets shine.
A grotto sings of ages past,
Where shadows linger, spells are cast.

The air is thick with fragrant moss,
A realm where time had known not loss.
In every crevice, stories weave,
Of magic born and souls that cleave.

Here faeries dwell, their laughter bright,
Illuminating the starry night.
With twinkling eyes, they flitter near,
And beckon all who dare to hear.

The roots hold whispers of the old,
In the soft earth, the tales unfold.
A gentle breeze, a fleeting sound,
In this enchanted space, we're bound.

Among the stones, the ages stir,
With every whisper, hearts concur.
In grottos deep, our dreams take flight,
As moonlight bathes the world in light.

Shadows of the Wildwood Realm

In shadowed glades where secrets dwell,
A wildwood realm casts its spell.
The trees stand tall, a silent guard,
As twilight weaves the night abraded.

Each rustling leaf, a tale unfolds,
Of ancient echoes and myths retold.
The forest sighs, a forgotten tune,
Underneath the watchful moon.

Creatures linger in twilight's haze,
Their eyes aglow in twilight's gaze.
A flicker, a howler, a whispered trace,
In wildwood shadows, we find our place.

The branches speak in hushed delight,
In every whisper, a spark of light.
With every step, the path grows clear,
Leading us to what we hold dear.

The wildwood breathes, a timeless call,
In shadows cast, we rise, we fall.
Embrace the night, the secrets swirl,
In shadows of this wildwood world.

Secrets Beneath the Forest Floor

In silence deep, beneath the ground,
Where magic sleeps, and dreams abound.
The roots entwine like whispered thoughts,
In hidden realms where beauty's caught.

Each pebble holds a timeless tale,
Of gentle streams and winds that sail.
In earthy beds, the secrets lie,
Of ancient trees that touch the sky.

The forest floor, a tapestry,
Of life and death, of what shall be.
In every shadow, a memory stays,
In every breeze, the past displays.

The stillness hums with life's refrain,
In sun-drenched spots, the joy, the pain.
Beneath our feet, the stories soar,
In secrets kept forevermore.

As roots connect to heart and soul,
The whispers rise, they make us whole.
In every step, the earth does sing,
Of life below, and all it brings.

Tracing Echoes in Thicket Dreams

In the thicket where shadows play,
Whispers gather like mist in the gray.
Dreams unravel in the soft moon's gaze,
Tracing secrets in a gentle haze.

Footsteps linger on the carpeted ground,
Echoes of laughter, a magical sound.
Each rustle tells tales of old,
Stories entwined in the dark and bold.

Branches weave in a mystical dance,
Inviting the heart to take a chance.
In the quiet, where magic spins,
Awakening wonders, around it begins.

Glimmering lights twinkle from afar,
A map of dreams written in stars.
The thicket breathes life to those who roam,
Cradling the wish to return home.

As dawn peeks through with a silken ray,
Thicket dreams gently drift away.
Yet the whispers remain, softly clear,
In the heart, forever held near.

Nightfall's Caress on Fabled Boughs

When night descends in velvet guise,
Boughs reach out to touch the skies.
A tender kiss from shadows deep,
Where ancient stories fall asleep.

Starlight dances on leaves so bright,
Cradled in the warmth of the night.
Chants of crickets weave a spell,
In the stillness, all is well.

The air is rich with secrets old,
Fables of courage and hearts so bold.
Under the moon's soft silver glow,
Whispers of wise ones, faint and slow.

Caressing boughs that sway and sway,
Guiding dreams that drift away.
In the darkness, magic thrives,
Where the spirit of wonder survives.

As dawn will chase the night's embrace,
Memories linger, time won't erase.
For in each moment, truth resides,
In nightfall's caress, where magic abides.

Sylvan Spirits in the Twilight Grove

In the grove where whispers sing,
Sylvan spirits, take to wing.
A waltz of shadows 'neath the trees,
A symphony stirred by the gentle breeze.

Golden hues paint the evening sky,
As day bids farewell with a soft sigh.
In the twilight, magic's embrace,
Leads wanderers to an enchanted place.

Murmurs of leaves share their delight,
While fireflies dance in the gathering night.
The spirits reflect in the twilight glow,
Guardians of tales we long to know.

With every step on the mossy ground,
A world of wonder is waiting to be found.
In harmony, with the murmured call,
The grove beckons, inspiring us all.

As eve's curtain falls with a soft sigh,
Sylvan spirits in shadows fly.
Carrying dreams to realms unseen,
In the twilight grove, forever serene.

The Veil of Thorns and Light

In a garden where shadows creep,
A veil of thorns, where secrets sleep.
Yet through the brambles, a shimmer glows,
A delicate dance where the heart knows.

Light weaves gently through jagged lace,
A path unfolds in a magical space.
While thorns may scratch, they tell a tale,
Of strength and courage that shall prevail.

Beneath the moon's watchful eye,
Blooming dreams in the night sky.
For every point that pierces skin,
A story of bravery begins within.

In the stillness, hope takes flight,
Amidst the struggles, burns a light.
The veil may shroud, but it cannot bind,
For every heart has the will to find.

Through thorns and shadows, we will tread,
Guided by the light ahead.
For every veil that hides delight,
Lies the promise of endless light.

Starlit Shadows and Woodland Charms

In twilight's grasp, the shadows dance,
Beneath the stars, they weave their chance.
Flecked with light, the forest sings,
Whispers soft of ancient things.

A glimmer wakes in emerald glades,
Where moonlit paths are softly laid.
The nightingale croons a gentle rhyme,
As dreams entwine in subtle time.

Old oaks stand guard, with wisdom vast,
While fleeting winds tell tales of the past.
Gleams of magic, both fierce and bright,
Twist through the shadows, cloaked in night.

Each rustling leaf whispers a clue,
Secrets held in the morning dew.
A dance of spirits, bright and rare,
Unfolds in the stillness, woven with care.

So linger here, 'neath the starlit sky,
Where hope flutters like a firefly.
In woodland charms of mystery spun,
The night awaits, and dreams have begun.

A Symphony of Sylvan Silence

In the quiet of the endless wood,
Where echoes linger, and shadows stood.
A symphony soft begins to rise,
As nature's heartbeat, softly sighs.

The whispering breeze, a gentle muse,
Calls forth the notes from the morning dues.
With every rustle, a tale unfolds,
Of forgotten dreams and legends told.

Underneath boughs of ancient trees,
The air dances with a fragrant breeze.
Woven in twilights that linger still,
Life pulses deep, beneath the hill.

A chorus of crickets sings at dusk,
In shadows thick where the wild things rust.
Glimmers of gold in a twilight brush,
Blend into the quiet, a soothing hush.

As night drapes the world in velvet blue,
The stars join in with a shimmering hue.
Join the silence, hear the night's embrace,
In the woodland's heart, find your place.

Captive Dreams in the Leafy Maze

In the heart of the leafy maze,
Where sunlight flecks in a golden blaze.
Dreams entwine like vines on a wall,
Calling to wanderers, one and all.

A path unfurls where the shadows play,
With secrets hidden along the way.
Soft sighs of an unseen breeze,
Carry whispers of the ancient trees.

Each turn conceals a magic fair,
Captive dreams suspended in the air.
Where laughter lingers, faint but near,
In the intertwining echoes here.

The brook babbles tales of those long gone,
As twilight paints the world in dawn.
A labyrinth of wonders, ripe with chance,
Inviting souls to join the dance.

So step inside the verdant spell,
Where stories bloom and shadows dwell.
In this maze of dreams, find your way,
And let your heart decide to stay.

Lament of the Twilight Wanderer

Underneath the soaring night,
The wanderer seeks the fading light.
Each step echoes with memories past,
A journey written in shadows cast.

With eyes that gleam like the stars above,
He roams the realms of lost love.
History whispers in the rustling leaves,
As the twilight weaves with what he believes.

A heart heavy with tales untold,
Yearns for warmth in the evening cold.
Yet through the gloom, a flicker of hope,
Guides the lost where the starlights slope.

The moonlight kisses the forest floor,
A haunting tune through the branches swore.
In every shiver of the night's embrace,
He searches still for a cherished place.

So tread lightly as twilight fades,
For each step holds a world that invades.
In the dance of shadows, sorrow is found,
A lament sung where the night knows no bound.

The Silken Tangle of Enchantment

In shadows deep where whispers dwell,
A tapestry of dreams to tell,
With silken threads of silver light,
They weave their spells in the dead of night.

Beneath the stars, where secrets hide,
The magic flows, a gentle tide,
Each knot and twist, a tale beguiled,
In the heart of the forest, fate's own child.

With every stitch, a wish takes flight,
Illuminating the darkest night,
Glimmers of hope in shadows cast,
In the silken tangle, enchantments last.

The moon unveils the hidden paths,
Where laughter echoes and time just laughs,
A dance of fireflies, a serenade,
In this enchanted realm, we're not afraid.

So dare to dream in the twilight hour,
Embrace the magic, its wondrous power,
For in each thread, a story resides,
A silken tangle where truth abides.

Beneath the Elder Tree's Embrace

In the shade of ancient bark we find,
Whispers of the past intertwined,
Beneath the elder's watchful gaze,
Time dances softly, a ghostly maze.

With roots that delve into the earth,
It cradles dreams since time of birth,
A shelter for the weary soul,
In its embrace, we feel whole.

The breeze carries tales from yesteryear,
Of laughter and joy mingled with fear,
As branches sway like a gentle hand,
Guiding us to a brighter land.

In twilight's glow, the world feels right,
Magic stirs in the fading light,
Each sigh of leaves, a serenade,
In the elder's embrace, worries fade.

So seek the wisdom of its shade,
Where dreams are sown and fears dismayed,
For beneath the elder's ancient heart,
We find our way, where all things start.

Lurking in the Gloom of Verdant Dreams

In the emerald depths where shadows creep,
Lurking secrets, in silence they sleep,
Whispers of magic, soft as a sigh,
Where spirits wander and wild things lie.

Beneath the canopy, where light refrains,
A world awakens, unbroken chains,
The rustle of leaves, a siren's call,
In verdant dreams, we rise and fall.

Ghostly figures dance through the trees,
Carried on the softest breeze,
With laughter lost in the weighty gloom,
They spin their stories, the tales of doom.

Yet in the darkness, a spark can gleam,
A glimmer of hope, a fleeting dream,
As night unfolds its velvet cloak,
In shadows deep, enchantments spoke.

So wander wisely through the mist,
In the verdant gloom, where wonders twist,
For what you seek may just reside,
In dreams alive, where worlds collide.

The Fae's Secret Tapestry

In glades where sunlight weaves its charm,
The fae create with gentle calm,
A tapestry spun from laughter light,
Delicate threads that shimmer bright.

Each color breathes a story true,
A whisper of skies in every hue,
With dainty stitches, they capture grace,
In every weave, a hidden place.

With petals soft, they form their art,
As nature sings and plays its part,
In patterns wild that shift and bend,
A magical dance that knows no end.

The fae, elusive, in shadows hide,
Guarding treasures of the other side,
Where dreams are stitched with love and care,
In a tapestry beyond compare.

So if you wander where the wild things roam,
Listen closely; you're near their home,
For in the weave, their secrets lie,
In the fae's tapestry, magic will sigh.

www.ingramcontent.com/pod-product-compliance
Ingram Content Group UK Ltd.
Pitfield, Milton Keynes, MK11 3LW, UK
UKHW021416220125
4239UKWH00007B/106